Unrequited Love

Cameron Cabral

BookLeaf
Publishing

India | USA | UK

Presentation by *BookLeaf Publishing*

Web: www.bookleafpub.com

E-mail: info@bookleafpub.com

ISBN: 9789357444064

First edition 2022

DEDICATION

To every chance I've been given,

and every opportunity I pursue.

ACKNOWLEDGEMENT

I'm extremely grateful for every relationship I've been in, regardless of how it turned out or ended. I'm grateful for the laughs, the memories, the long nights, the deep talks, the thrill, and so much more. I wouldn't change a thing.

I would also like to thank Caitlin Kelly for many of her books such as "The Words I Wish I Said", and "The Words of a Madman", as I have taken inspiration from her unique writing style. Her words hit me with such force that truly make me feel something deep inside, and I love how her simplicity in writing can have such a big impact.

PREFACE

Hopeless romantic. I would call myself this word for years like it had no meaning. Like I was proud, almost. I guess in a way I thought that being a hopeless romantic would make me stand out. I suppose I just naturally assumed every girl wants a high school boy who is truly lovely, not just amorous, someone who sees beyond what's just on the outside. However, I don't think I truly am the person I envisioned myself as. Maybe before the relationship I was.

I never actually thought to wonder, what happens after you get the girl. No one warns you about drowning under the constant voices in your head, wondering "what if she-". No one warns you about jealousy. Or how to depend on yourself. Or how to believe you're good enough. Or control.

No one warned me about how to be in an unrequited relationship. But I tried.

never good enough

I'm so hopelessly desperate
to be loved by you

not because,
I need to be loved,
or want your validation

not because,
I want to show you,
I'm worth your time

not because,
I crave the attention,
you never gave me

but because,
I need to prove to myself,
that I'm worth being loved

by someone like you.

stay

I constantly find myself missing you
& the way things used to be.
Thinking about all of our memories
what could have been, if you didn't leave.

I think of what I could have changed,
& all the words I wish I said.
While I lie alone in the silence,
staring at the ceiling from my bed.

Maybe one day we'll meet again, perhaps
in some coffee shop on a warm summer day.
Or maybe we aren't meant to be at all,
no matter how much I beg for you to stay.

regret

oh how I wished this time would be different
I had such high hopes, for you & I
but I guess I fucked it up like always
so you had no other choice but to say goodbye

after a while I start to question
how many times I can endure this pain
I don't think I can take another heartbreak
I'm so tired of being played like a game

additionally

do me a favor.
in another life,
hurt me a little more.

moving on would be so much easier.

dazed

I loved you so much
that despite the way
you made me be

I still found a way to
sympathize, and justify
everything you did to me

unknown

6

maybe if I told you I loved you
before it was too late
we'd be together, happy
and my mind would be in a good state.

power

the control you
have over me
is frightening

you made me feel so selfish
for wanting to receive the love
I gave to you
without even trying

But the worst part is,
all it takes is a
disguise of effort
and I bend to your will
before blinking

blinded

I didn't want to be right
I didn't really think you did it
but I was and you did
you just didn't want to admit it

you lead me along a lie
making me look like a fool
you made me feel so ruptured
like you were just using me as a tool

but I kept my head down low
and put on the mask I knew so well
I've lost too many people in my life
and I couldn't just bid you farewell

forgotten

I can't remember your face anymore,
or your laugh, eyes, or smile
& while a part of me knows I'm better off
I just wish you would've stayed awhile.

late at night

every night
I resist the
urge to send
you the text
"I miss you"

because I know you could
never send it back.

self hatred

that loud overbearing noise
consumes every thought in my head
kicking me down to the ground
making me wish I were dead

no matter how many times I apologize
the sight of your tears is plenty
to make me realize I'm the monster
leaving me to feel so empty

in another life

I hope in another life
our love story lasts a little longer
and we are a little less broken

I hope in another life
the voice in your head doesn't hold you back
from reaching your full potential

I hope in another life
our love is passionate and intimate
rather than subliminal and imperceptible

in another life I know,
you and I,
we're perfect for each other

guilt

you tell me you love me
and I say it back
but my insides start to hurt
and I feel a sort of lack

why does this happen to me
why can't my feelings stay true
I don't want to break your heart
I don't want to hurt you

the voice in my head is overwhelming
knowing your love is superior
because my stupid-self doesn't want it
and that voice makes me feel inferior

philanthropical

while I hope you never experience
the pain you put my through
I hope one day you understand
everything I did for you.

I know you were young
and I tried my best to teach you
but turns out I was unexperienced as well
and I needed to be taught how to love, too.

everyday I wish I could go back
knowing now how to love and last
but I guess you look happier now
and the past is in the past.

right person wrong time

I don't think there's anything more tragic
than loving the right person at the wrong time.

what if, perhaps, you & I are meant to be?
we are just too young, too ignorant to know it.

& by the time we are older,
we've already moved on in our lives

when all along we belong together
we just don't know that, now.

touch

it was a quick and harmless moment,
when my hand grazed past yours
you didn't think much of it, I'm sure
you carried on your way,
never thinking to give me the
time of day
meanwhile it keeps me awake for hours
wondering if you're feeling what I feel too
it's so tragic to love someone
while they never even think of you

doubt

you dropped me
like I was nothing
& kept going on with life.

was anything we had real?
did I even mean anything to you?
was I not good enough?
did I come off too strong?
how could I have changed?

just tell me why,
please I need to know
what did I do to fuck it up this time?

end

& that last look we gave each other
knowing it would be the last time,
that look spoke a thousand words of it's own.

& now my words left unsaid,
will haunt me forever.